A high spirited romp with language and a tough spiritual struggle with suffering, violence, the text of the Old Testament, and a God who explains that "Heaven is everyone armed and open carry. Come on in." Finishing this book I turned right around and started over—it was that rich, that good.

—Alicia Ostriker

Author of *Waiting for the Light* and *The Volcano and After*

Sleeping as Fast as I Can is a book where prayers are filled with history, and history is filled with the urgency of the present; a book that isn't afraid of tragedy because it holds music as a shield. For me, Michelson's poems deliver an unrelenting message, one unafraid to transport "home our holy, temporary hearts."

—Ilya Kaminsky

Author of *Deaf Republic* and *Dancing in Odessa*

Richard Michelson's poems are easy to read and hard at the same time. With clarity and wit their honesty touches deep into pain: of a father lost long ago, of a mother now in her decline, of life, of contemporary history, of Jewish life, of Jewish history, of the violence that spoils it all. But then come the words of blessing in the midst of the dark that understands "Light is our only future."

—Rodger Kamenetz

Author of *The Missing Jew: Poems 1976-2022*

Richard Michelson is a poet who understands the measure and music in the art of poetry. *Sleeping as Fast as I Can* brings prayers, rants, memoria, and rage against hatred, violence, racism, and anti-Semitism in a bitches brew of language on every page. . . .

—Patricia Spears Jones

Author, *A Lucent Fire: New and Selected Poems*

Sleeping as Fast as I Can

Sleeping as Fast as I Can

Poems

RICHARD MICHELSON

BOOKS

SLEEPING AS FAST AS I CAN
Poems

Slant Books
P.O. Box 60295
Seattle, WA 98160

www.slantbooks.org

Cataloguing-in-Publication data:

Names: Michelson, Richard.
Title: Sleeping as fast as i can: poems / Richard Michelson.
Description: Seattle, WA: Slant Books, 2023
Identifiers: ISBN 978-1-63982-136-5 (hardcover) | ISBN 978-1-63982-135-8 (paperback) | ISBN 978-1-63982-137-2 (ebook)
Subjects: LCSH: American poetry | American poetry—21st century | American poetry—Jewish authors | Jewish religious poetry, English

For Jennifer (still, again, and ever)

Do you see that arch over there from the Roman period? It doesn't matter, but near it, a little to the left and then down a bit, there's a man who has just bought fruit and vegetables for his family.
—Yehuda Amichai

Sleep faster, we need the pillows!
—Yiddish folk saying

Contents

III Reading Kafka to My Daughter

IV Turtle of Slow Devotion

Coda

Prelude

Today, let us approach the divine like this elephant lumbering
toward the prepared blank canvas. Let us surround ourselves
with pails of paint, and plunge our delicate noses directly into
the gelatinous rainbow. O dainty Boom Rod, mischievous Paya,
have I not flown above clouds these twenty-something-odd-hours
to arrive on the unknown side of the heavens. O cheerful Chong,
I draw near you, knowing full well the parable of the blind monks,
all six of them stumbling to understand how the sighted can label
what we see as The Truth. For who among us does not desire
inspiration, or to leave our faint mark on white paper. But let me,
if only this hour, dare to stand apart from the good-hearted people,
these well-intentioned foreign tourists who want so badly to believe
in your pachyderm paintings, and the eternal uplifting power of art
that they'll ignore the soft tissue of your outer ear, the sharp hook
hidden in the handler's left hand, his right controlling your tusks
until attention drifts to our own self-portraits, or some distant god.

I

A Pitying of Turtledoves

PRAYER

Today, I am weary of my soul, forever dragging behind me,
clanging for attention like tin cans left tied to a coupe fender
long after the sacred vows. Just now another Black motorist
murdered live on YouTube (shared, copied, spread virally),
tomorrow an Asian, Tuesday a Jew; O friends, transgender,
and cis, what imagination would lash raw ankles to exhaust-
pipes, turn the key and hit the gas? In Rembrandt's *Flayed Ox*,
he's mixed bits of lampblack into the ochre and burnt umber;
and on my Louvre *lune de miel,* I observed once more a desire
to make the grotesque beautiful. Are we here to be God's body,
or God's language? O composers, in what key do we set cruelty?
O poets, what rhymes with the rape of a child? While wildfires
out west melt flesh and southern hurricanes scream the word
mercy, shall we pray by the side of this road my love; my Lord?

POISONING THE WELL

It was 1348 when the Toulon Jews were first accused
of poisoning wells, my grandfather says. I've refused,

at eight, to wash my hands before dinner, and so a story
about purity, the bubonic plague, and God's glory

is proper punishment; though then as now, persecution
and rotting cadavers seemed to me meager confirmation

of heavenly endorsement. When brutalized, some reach
toward religion; others might apostatize or research

their inner demons. My grandfather abandoned all trivial
delights for Talmudic law; bathing corpses before burial,

purging the house of *chametz* and *kashering* the oven
each Pesach, while I, feather in hand, dusted for leaven.

The city's Jews, segregated in a walled-off ghetto, escaped
pestilence only to face forced repentance or, scape-

goated, to be staked and burned. I think of those pious
today on hearing the President cite a "Chinese virus"

to stoke fear, while trumpeting ignorance. The mobs
attacked to absolve debts, embezzle land, or appease gods.

What fears, I wonder, will my grandchildren understand me to be quelling, when I demand they wash their hands?

THE WEDDING IN THE CEMETERY

The wedding in the cemetery featured scripture, loud
music, two rabbis, and the bride dressed in a shroud

my grandfather tells me. He's inching toward the heart
of his lecture, while I'm composing *till death do us part*

punchlines, my pre-teen self not yet grasping the subtext
or the year. 1918, he repeats, the Spanish Flu infecting

a third of the world's population, already fifty million
dead and in my grandfather's Polish shtetl, superstition

has brought hundreds graveside to congratulate the groom.
I think of this now while watching my niece wed via Zoom,

her plans amended by today's pandemic; rabbi-by-remote
reciting sacred rites, relatives clicking the thumbs up emoji

or the clapping hands, as ancient Hebraic prayers appear
scrolling across a six-foot flat-screen TV. *Love, not fear*

must triumph, my grandfather says once again, as I suffer
one fortune-cookie aphorism after another. Someone offers

an on-line toast and we raise imaginary glasses. *L'chaim*
still reverberates off of every broken headstone. *I Am*

That I Am, God tells the assembled. *Pity the living guests,* the dead jest, *who believe themselves amongst the blessed.*

BLESS YOU

Since sneezing was the first sign of falling ill with the plague,
Pope Gregory ordered prayer for divine intercession.

Gesundheit, great-aunt Frida calls out, each sneeze
another occasion for my soul to abandon my body.
I hurry my index finger under my nose horizontally
blocking both nostrils as tutored, so evil can't seize
an inhale to fill the void. *Denying the devil his due,*
Frida dubs it, she who, at sixty to my six, reflexively
worries her brow, reaches toward a box of Kleenex,
and spits over her shoulder. I mimic *ptui, ptui, ptui.*
Tonight, eight years older than she was at her death,
and dining curbside to curtail the coronavirus, I hear,
two tables over, *ah-choo,* and for the first time in years
measure the distance between superstition and truth.
Around me panic, as, mid-forkful, everyone freezes.
May God keep us up-wind from all airborne diseases.

LUCKY JEW GHAZAL

Lucky Jew figurines are more popular and populous than actual Jews in Poland.
    —*Times of Israel*

In my kiosk in Krakow, you can buy a Lucky Jew.
Good fortune vows to follow you who own this tchotchke Jew.

Placed near the entry door, he's sure to keep your coins secure.
This knick-knack makes you well-to-do just like a wealthy Jew.

Rub his kippah, stroke his beard, or tug his curly sidelocks.
Your stocks will increase faster than a billion-zloty Jew's.

Long life and prosperity are how Jews bless their brethren.
They dress in black. Stay in the pink. Think like a healthy Jew.

Jewish prophets have a nose for profit and success.
Contrast your prospects with my needing-rhinoplasty Jews.

A rabbit foot, or horseshoe charm won't cause you any harm,
but each one lacks the ear of G-d, so try my tax-free Jews.

Jews are resourceful, clever, kindly; that is why good news
pursues even the socialist or bourgeois Bernie Jews.

I beg you, Richard, don't pass by this poor unlucky Jew.
Put up your nose and mock me then; rich fucking lucky Jew.

VERMIN

It was essential, Einstein stated, that he bring his violin
to Berta Fanta's salon on Prague's Old Town Square.
It is 1912, four years until Relativity, and six before
the first wave of the Spanish flu will kill, among the
500 million infected, the painter, Egon Schiele, already
despondent over the death, three days earlier, of his lover,

Edith, and their unborn child. Painting his pregnant lover
the day before her death he could already hear the viola
and mournful bassoon of Mozart's Requiem Mass. Ready
now to sketch himself dying, he gazes into the small square
of his shaving mirror, and recalls how he first entered the
Vienna Academy of Fine Arts at age sixteen, even before

his initial shave, no younger student accepted before
or since. He died, never to know he'd won that spot over
the seventeen-year-old Adolph Hitler, who'd later loathe
"degenerate art" and "physicist Jews," moving to Berlin
to pursue politics, aborting both brush and pen. The square-
root-of-time displacing millennia-of-atoms is music already

usurping Einstein's brain as, nodding to Max Brod, he readies
his violin under his chin. The pianist, who already has four
of his 83 books penned to literary acclaim, looks squarely
into the eyes of his closest friend, Franz Kafka. Brod loves
his quiet companion's unpublished scribblings, which violate
all of fiction's conventions. He had offered Franz absinthe

for courage before inviting him to Berta's if he'd recite the
story about a transformation into vermin. Yet, rising to read
to his fellow Jews, even Kafka cannot conceive of violence
so extreme that each present will be dubbed a cockroach. For
now, though, let's leave these imaginative culture-lovers
in paradise; and in a Kafkesque absurdity of E=MC squared,

time travel to British Columbia where we'll reappear squarely
inside a brothel owned by Bavarian born Friedrich Trump. The-
oretically viable, we can locate the villain who, full of self-love,
emigrated at sixteen to avoid the military draft. He has already
planned a move to Queens, where he'll die five months before
Schiele of the same deadly flu, his atoms still infecting us via

his grandson's love of Hitlerian speech; even Kafka cannot square
anti-alien taunts with Melania's *Einstein-visa* violation. *I pray Thee
Lord,* a fevered Mozart pleads; *forgive me, forget me, I am done for.*

FAKE NEWS

"My throte is kut unto my nekke boon"

When the President's spokesperson coined the term *alternative facts*
to replace *blatant lies,* my Facebook feed went crazy. I'm writing a poem
titled "Fake News" one "friend" said, but another cautioned: "Too topical;
it'll be fish-wrap in days and no one will know what you're posting about."
But I'm still contemplating St. William of Norwich, the apprentice tanner
found dead in the twelfth century near the corner of Cruelty and Credulity
while the monk, Thomas of Monmouth, concocted a blood libel, blaming
the ritual murder—*to flavor their matzo*—on the Jews; Martyred, the boy
would end up on this panel of painted oak in London's Victoria and Albert,
where I'm sitting on a bench checking my brand-new Verizon smartphone
for the latest evidence supporting my political views. I'm reading clickbait
instead of *The Canterbury Tales,* so not till later, will I recall that Chaucer,
two hundred years after, would spread the same vile libel through the lips
of his Prioress; her prologue, a much more persuasive and timeless fiction.

GOSSIP IS FORBIDDEN

the Rabbi said, peering over his bifocals. If you steal goods
or money you can repent and repay, but not so the evil tongue.
Permission to shoplift is what we, at fifteen, heard, high-fiving
outside the synagogue door. Catch us if you can—we'll atone
in fifty years if any one of us is left alive. Today at sixty-five
I see three teens pocketing chocolates from the neighborhood

bodega, stuffing their stylish kangaroo-pouch Patagonia hoodies
with ninety-two percent dark Ghirardelli plus boxes of Good
& Plenty pink candy. I start to speak, then, biting my tongue,
wind it back into the clammy dankness of its mucosa-lined cave.
One boy turns, sees me seeing and freezes until the ringtone
of his iPhone breaks the spell. The tableau instantly comes alive,

each of us playing our part. And you, dear reader, who are still alive,
need to know that in The Year of Our Lord, 2017, white-hooded
hoodlums marched through Charlottesville, Virginia, intoning
Jew will not replace us and our President said there were "good
and bad apples, bigots and very fine people" on either side. Tongue-
tied, I cannot believe what my ears have heard so I replay those five

words again in my mind: *Jew will not replace us.* When I was five,
my grandfather reprimanded my first-grade schoolmates with five
words of his own: *Words hurt worse than stones.* His mother tongue
shamed me with its Yiddish-accented appeal to the brotherhood
of White America. I'd already heard *Christ-killer, kike,* and the Good
Friday prayer for the "perfidious Jews." For years I spoke a monotone

to distance myself from those excitable Semites whose dark skin tones
proved—until it didn't—then did again—that they would never be saved.
A curse could kill, my grandmother knew, so she stayed silent at Good-
Will working us into the mainstream, her prayers parting seas, saving
us with each penny saved. Thank God she didn't live to see us all hood-
winked. Behind the bars of her teeth, guarded by lips, her tongue,

locked up like a murderer serving a life sentence, stills my own tongue
as these three boys saunter down the aisle. Defying the overtones
of racism—two Latino, one Black—the Pakistani earning his livelihood
behind the counter pulls out a gun. And here again we freeze, all five
posed like a Ghirlandaio fresco, when, from the mouth of the cave,
Jesus, resurrected, walks through the open door. I bring you The Good

News, he babbles, speaking in tongues. He picks up and pockets a Good
Land apple. O, my undocumented Rabbi, I intone, what parable can save
us? *Beresh't was falsehood and truth, he says. Speak, my child, and live.*

ON VIEWING THE CARDBOARD PIG WITH THE STAR OF DAVID AT THE DEFUND THE POLICE/BLACK LIVES MATTER RALLY

Looking around the demonstration, surrounded by older White
liberals like myself chanting *Black Lives Matter* after the murder
of George Floyd, I realize today is the date of my father's murder
more than forty years ago, not by knee or knife, but the hot White

fury of a single bullet from a stolen gun. The drug-addicted Black
man—really still a boy—can barely steady himself to run. My father,
the last Jewish shopkeeper in a once Black, newly Latino neighbor-
hood long abandoned by police—*let them all kill each other; Black,*

or Brown—who gives a shit—would not recognize himself as White
or comprehend *privilege. Pig-Dog,* names my dehumanized father's
father stitched into the yellow stars of the ghetto's dirty-Jew squalor
so his son's son—me—might someday earn my all-American White-

collar legal credentials. Instead, I grew up idolizing Baraka's Black
Arts Movement, Baldwin's Blues, cheering the arm-in-arm colors
marching behind Rev King and Reb Heschel as Bull Connor orders
his cops to attack with dogs and guns and clubs. Too soon, Baraka

blaming Jews for 9-11, each club admitting only its own, while White
supremacists arm themselves, waiting. *Be neither saint nor martyr*
I beg my son, another virus-masked New Yorker, while my daughter
occupies the corner of Gentrification & Squalor, her transgender-Black

allies demanding unconditional love. O America with your White-washed past, five-pointed stars, and stiff-backed pigs led to slaughter, how can I remember the names of the dead? Look, there's my father. *Today I am Floyd,* he prays. *Barukh ata Adonai. Today I am Black.*

IN PRAISE OF DISORDER

I.

Let us praise the rabbis disrupting traffic in front of Trump Tower
to protest the ban on Muslim immigration, all nineteen arrested
for disorderly conduct. Praise, also, the tired police officer offering
gently the cuff, as the television reporters jostle for a better position.
Let us honor, too, the lives of those stuck in gridlock, this one cursing
clerics in general, that one Arabs and Jews only, the devil take them
both; she leans on her horn, lacking not sympathy for the just cause,
she'll explain one day to her daughter, but just because, now late
for spin class, she must message the babysitter, and call the dogwalker,
who rearranges his own plans, postponing a right-swiped date who will
never text back, and was she the love he'd spent his life waiting for?

II.

Let us applaud, now, the small disorders; a wine glass set to the left
of the Seder plate, the fork positioned to the far right of the knife,
upsetting expectations and forcing the wrong hand to overreach.
Kudos too, to the fifteen-line sonnet and the sixteen-syllable haiku.
But let us not dishonor the perfect rows in which Korczak marched
his trusting, if unsuspecting army of orphans into the welcoming arms
of the gas chamber. Did they not, in their minds, enter less orderly
than the swarming and angry multitudes that followed Moses?

III.

It is because of that which the LORD did for me when I came out of Egypt
that God ordered each Jew to tell their children of the escape from slavery.
And so, the hand-washing must precede the *karpas* and the breaking
of the middle matzo in the one and perfect order, until the story is complete.
In this way, we too follow our ancestors like an endless *renga*, each stanza
shifting the meaning of the generations before. Which of the Four Sons
would you like to recite? my grandfather asks. He is so still in his chair,
his posture extols his addiction to constancy, his skill at memorization.
Shall I be Wise, Wicked, Simple, or the child who does not even know
how to question? Let us praise those unable or unwilling to choose.

VENERY: A PRAYER

Tree of Life Synagogue, Squirrel Hill—10/27/18

I.

A convocation of eagles
A business of flies
A clattering of jackdaws
A parliament of owls
A congregation of plovers

II.

A scurry of squirrels
A destruction of cats
A leash of foxes
An ambush of tigers
A murder of Jews

III.

An army of ants
A nest of vipers
A bellowing of bullfinches
A scold of jays
A deceit of lapwings
A pitying of turtledoves

IV.

Joyce Jew
Richard Jew
Rose Jew
Jerry Jew
Cecil Jew
David Jew
Bernice Jew
Sylvan Jew
Daniel Jew
Melvin Jew
Irving Jew

V.

A shepherd of gays
An inflammation of immigrants
A molestation of Catholics
A bullet of Black boys
An anguish of mothers
A coward of congressmen
A plague of martyrs
A martyr of angels

OPEN CARRY

After Pittsburgh, what would you have me do, God asks?
Eleven slaughtered in my own living room. And that cute
Black kid, what was his/her name? No, the other one. No,
the other one. No, not that one. Damn, never mind. Maybe
I should have gone with metal detectors, but the beeping
interfered with the harpists. What about Auschwitz? Not
many of you remember that but for me a million years is
less than a second. Imagine tough Jews with guns guard-
ing the ghetto. I just thought of that joke your father liked.
A poor man begs me for a billion dollars. Lord, for you it
isn't even a penny. OK, I say, in a minute. I didn't mean
to mention your dad. That must've been tough back then,
him gunned down for being. . . . Me, I don't see color, race,
or sexual orientation. I am what your world calls a white
limousine liberal. Sorry, I know, not funny. Even as a little
god I'd guffaw in all the wrong places. Ever get the giggles
at a funeral? That's the devil's laughter spewing like an AK-
47 in a schoolyard. Don't let Satan fool you, pretending He's
me. Heaven is everyone armed and open carry. Come on in.

THE EIGHTH NIGHT

A bullet behind the Gates of Heaven; one angel has fallen,
another fleeing. *Higher pickets*, God promises, *wider posts.*
I worry again for my father, fifty years dead, and still lost
in schematics of achievable security; nightly muscling steel
heavy-duty sectional doors, setting the alarm, before dialing
home from the corner booth so Ma knew to heat our dinners.
Tonight, every candle lit; a tiny inferno through which sinners
and too few saints ever ascend. *During my previous miracles*
God complains, *didn't I light the way?* Yes, these nine flames,
I answer, are our only answer. Yesterday, more Jews murdered,
two meals interrupted by domestic terrorists, would-be-martyrs
in pursuit of viral video. Pay attention, my father, still-scheming,
exclaims; in three days, a new decade, hope, a flicker of rebirth.
Praise God who tracked the culprits, expelled them back to earth.

THE FLOOD

In the synagogue above the synagogue with the active shooter
God is studying for God's Bar-Mitzvah. First, He invents Time—
the second Shabbat after Simchat Torah—to know which *parshah*
to chant. Next, create Language. *White-nationalist, hate-crime,*
my mother echoes, the senior-living facility TV blaring, dementia
of toxic proteins attacking the shrunken furrows of her brain.
In today's verse God wipes out the wicked, sparing only Noah,
his three sons, their blameless beasts and unnamed wives as rain-
bows of blood and urine splatter the sanctuary wall; the *bimah*
abandoned but for the slain Rabbi. Once, my mother parsed fables
for us kids: rapture as scripture's symptom and cause. *Kumbaya,*
she hums now, softly, as the aide leads her toward the ladies' table
for lunch, their stares blank as teenage sociopaths' in the aftermath
of revenge. O mourners, divinely warned, we are drowning in faith.

SMOKE

is pouring from God's computer. Who here will help? It's Sunday
morning at the Mall of America, and all the technicians are still
at church; security is loading pellet guns—their bi-weekly drill
pursuing active-shooter actors. Density approaches infinity
as the mist lifts from the motherboard and obscures the screen.
Elephants hold their trunks high above the tree line gasping for air.
The ovens of Sobibor, Hiroshima, Nine-Eleven, cannot compare
to the fumes rising from God's mainframe. O angels, even heaven
is burning with its burnished gates double bolted from the inside.
When the bullet entered the black abyss of the child's body
like a collapsing star swallowing its surroundings, the energy
emitted swirled bright as a hydrogen fire. Who here will survive
the blinding incandescence of the event horizon? Blessed mother,
blessed animal sacrifice, escape is futile. Light is our only future.

ANGELS WITH GUNS GUARDING
THE GATES OF HEAVEN

The only thing that stops a bad guy with a gun is a good guy with a gun.
   —National Rifle Association CEO Wayne LaPierre

The angel staying the dagger-raised-arm of Abraham was
one of the good guys. But studying, again, *Isaac's Binding*,
painted after Rembrandt, age twenty-nine, suffered his first-
born son's death, I find no weapon hidden beneath the wings
of God's blue cloaked go-between. And what to make of Jacob
wrestling—hand to hand combat—with his better nature? Faith
was all they had in common. Even Rubens's Lucifer-led rebels,
in their fallen orgy of luscious flesh, had only their foolish
Flemish selves to censure. So, when the president's election
committee dubbed as "angels" those who had lost loved ones
to violence by illegal South American refugees, I wondered
which side of the border wall between heaven and hell was left
to climb. I was in La Paz, Bolivia when I came upon the Master
of Calamarca's *Archangel Asiel with Rifle* which I learned
from the department of tourism, spawned a convention of gun-
toting deities throughout the Andes: Christ's army protecting
the faithful. The missionary-enforced Catholicism banned
the practice of pre-Hispanic religions and *the indigenous Inca*
thought Spanish firepower supernatural. My grandmother didn't
live to see her youngest son, my father, murdered in a Brooklyn
gutter by a fifth generation, drug-addicted, unemployed house-
painter whose ancestors were dragged here like devils in chains.
If there were armed guards inside the temple, the president said,

25

after his white nationalist supporter slaughtered eleven in Pittsburgh,
they would have been able to stop him. Today, I enter the unlocked
door of my Amherst synagogue, once the church where Emily
Dickinson also attempted to pray. The light pours through the
sanctuary's stained-glass windows, and squinting, I see shadows
positing a loaded gun in the poet's hand. We are all father Abraham
and also, Isaac the son, she explains. And I confess how once
I, too, believed that a guardian angel walked before each of us,
unarmed, and chanting: *Make Way for The Image of The Lord.*

II

Temporary Hearts

NEIGHBORHOOD VILLANELLE

In this neighborhood you'd better learn to fight,
my father says. Real schooling's from hard knocks.
Books won't save your life. He knows I'd rather write

and read. I don't talk back. His love is no birthright.
Instead, I bluff, act tough. He teaches me to box.
In this neighborhood you'd better learn to fight,

he says, or you'll be prey; better tough Israelite
than studious Black Hat, defenseless Orthodox.
Books won't save your life. I know you'd rather write.

Next day was Hanukkah, the Festival of Lights.
"Hey Jew-Boy," some kids jeered (as if I wore earlocks).
I was no Maccabee. Bluff called, I could not fight.

I came to battered, bruised, but had no appetite
for bloodshed or revenge. Instead, I walked for blocks,
prayed books would save my life. I swore someday I'd write

these lines. And now I have. We never kissed goodnight
yet every poem I wrote, he saved. The paradox:
a bullet stopped his life; lead plug he could not fight.
I escape the neighborhood with every word I write.

MAYBE THE MESSIAH

Maybe the Messiah not coming is proof enough, Kafka chalks
across the board, *that God exists.* He's subbing my eighth-grade
math class, but I'm still not convinced that multiplying negatives
equals a positive, or that anyone understands the evidence
of absence: the dark matter of my father's murder; mother,
at home, reaching for the rotary, her spine quivering

like my oscilloscope's needle. Maybe the Messiah can explain
how atoms once breathed out by Aristotle ended up in the algorithms
of A.A. Michelson as he measured the speed of light.
How fast must the superhero of myself travel to go back in time
to tackle the gunman or deflect the bullet that altered my family's future.
But already the bell's crying *physics* and Kafka's screening the film

about the butterfly that caused the avalanche on the other side
of the world. It's called the theorem of unintended consequences,
but you might know it better as just bad luck. *Listen,* Kafka says,
stop beating yourself up. And suddenly he's clapping erasers
and flapping his arms like my mother demonstrating the myth
of the Messiah, or an angel disappearing in a storm cloud of dust.

A HORSE CURE

is what Munch called it when he scattered his canvases outside
in the snow, or set them under the blazing sun, their resilience
tested like Spartan children blindfolded in foreign pastures,
forced to find a path home. I see, framed by her picture window,
my mother at ninety-three, stretched out on a chaise lounge
in the South Florida heat, and I can imagine how the colors
in those paintings faded over time until scarcely an outline
remained; but their power preserved like the soul's energy
after the body's death. Today, as I gather together the stacks
of books I've read but barely remember, and set them back
on my mind's shelf, next to the volumes of poems faithlessly
abandoned, I wonder if maybe this life is less about survival
of the fittest than each of us finding our own horse cure,
that immaculate moment when we put down the brush and allow
luck or chance to take control. I watch now, as my mother sets
aside her newspaper and pencil, struggling dizzily to her feet,
untroubled by phrases left unfinished, the puzzle incomplete.

LIFE SENTENCE

A life sentence is what was handed down to the thief
that gunned down your father, my mother said,
her breathing labored, as if by hammering words—tread
and riser—into a flight of stairs, she could climb past grief,
ascending up and out of her own history. Gunned down,
she repeats, for ten dollars and half a tuna sandwich.
The briefcase, an open disappointment, tossed in a ditch
and found, infested with fingerprints, each a proper noun
announcing, like an intricately hand-lettered calling card,
the murderer's name and table number. To set the scene
for her story, my mother drops metaphor—*at seventeen
I married the boy next door*—as we exit the graveyard,
down three steps, me stumbling on the bottom one, broken
and forgotten, like a life unwritten, its sentences unspoken.

LIFE SENTENCE

It's like speed dating at a mortician's convention,
my mother explains; the first sentence must awe, wow,
or shock; entertain, or risk a reader's waning attention
before truth's modest list of achievements. It's only now
I understand that the creative writing seminar I insisted
she join at the assisted living facility (*Elevator to Heaven*)
has cast her as entrepreneur, and God as venture capitalist;
sixty seconds to make her eternal pitch—as though even
the afterlife can't improve upon our uninspired dreams
of everlasting success. Enough plot, or too literary?
she asks, reading from her initial draft; which seems
a peculiar question while composing one's obituary.
But for now, she's alert and focused as she revises text,
laboring her life into art, undeterred by what comes next.

WHAT MY MOTHER REMEMBERS—MEMORIAL DAY

Me, as of today. And my wife, when we're together. Both kids,
though not whose kids they are. The once bright patterned Picasso
kitchen wallpaper with its slap-dash daubs of blue and yellow.
Mostly she's haunting her teenaged self. She lowers both eyelids
to better remember a scene, although the plot is long forgotten,
as if her life were God's first draft, and only random passages
remain. Suddenly, she laughs, recollecting the mixed-up letters;
my father's folded aerogram addressed to her fiancé stationed
overseas—my existence based on that single error. Her marriage
is ever present, but she can't recall her husband's murder. It takes
a lifetime, Picasso said, to learn to splatter like a child. Mistakes
once mattered, but memory must be the narrative she's rearranged
now that she can no longer color within lines. She has no quarrel
anymore with time; its loss, she seems to say, is sorrow's cure-all.

HERE I AM

—October 10th

The bouncer at Club Canaan could be God guarding
the heavenly gates; inscrutable rules, sudden flashes
of dumb muscle, occasional mercy. *Ashes to ashes,*
he murmurs, waving an underage in, without carding.
My father would insist she was outfitted for trouble—
pierced tongue, pearl studs, the flat logic of spiked heels
lifting her nearer to rapture; but he's missing the details
engraved on our granite invitation. We are all the shovel
moving small mounds of earth into our own open graves.
We are all too young and driving too fast. We're Asian,
Black, and Jew. We're full of sin and cancer. Here I am
writing again about my father's murder, as he saves me
my place in line. Today, he'd have turned ninety-five.
The miracle isn't life, he argues. It's having been alive.

I CREATE AS I SPEAK

The difference between this soothing south Caribbean breeze
and my Florida-gulf gale-force concrete-crushing jackhammer
of air demolishing your mother's condominium is only an error
of grammar, God says, as if stars weren't matter, but apologies
for darkness; as if the same winds didn't once level Babel.
In the shelter, routine disrupted, my mother's mind prepares
to exit the earth before her essence acquiesces. She shares
the silences of grandfather's goldfish: Celan, Adorno, Abel,
each named in honor of their wide-eyed accusations. Look
how their tiny mouths open and close, obliterating nothing.
Let my prayers be that ineffective. Let me fold my mother's
frail and failing body into the sheets of this too narrow cot
as carefully as rage nestled deep inside of her encouragement.
The puzzles you fed me, mother, are still my nourishment.

MOSES EVERYWHERE

First thing this morning, he's crossing the crowded causeway,
pausing mid-stride to conduct his silent music. I'm praying
for a break in the traffic, when miraculously, the cars part
and he wanders beyond my hotel window's view. Dear God,
I call out, how do you choose among us? And here, he reappears
but slow of tongue and years younger, hiding within the heart
of this prideful princeling following home the prison guard
who'd beaten his older brother. I'm in the courthouse, paying
my contested parking ticket when the verdict is handed down
and the accused sentenced to death for murder. Even drowning
in the rising waters before sleep, I hear him in the feeble prayer
of my mother. Bring me home, she pleads, from her cradled cot
in the Senior Care facility. Please. I'm begging. Florida's too hot.
Tomorrow, I promise. But I shalt not. I shalt never. I shalt not.

ENVISIONING THE LIFE, POST-PAROLE, OF MY FATHER'S MURDERER

Rainbows exist, the nurse explains, not in the troposphere,
but only on the viewer's retina. Then, staring at her iPhone
as if it housed time, or regret, she excuses herself. Alone
til my pupils dilate and the doctor arrives, I have leisure
to ponder how doubt can enter the eye socket of the body
like a bullet, instantly upsetting the moneylender's table,
and scattering the interior architecture of belief until, unable
to breathe, we lie down like Paschal lambs. *Holy, Holy. Holy*
we chant, repeating the lies our ancestors sang before death.
Behind bars, you found Jesus, Krishna, Mohammed, Buddha.
Your debt paid, I have come to welcome you to your future.
Here, *soul* is named for the breath that breaks from our mouths
after a sucker punch to the gut; and God's multicolored coat,
which we call *truth*, still costs less than a shave, and a haircut.

WHAT MY MOTHER REMEMBERS—NEW YEAR'S DAY

My QuickBooks app automatically updates, announces
in all-caps orange: OVER-BUDGET. I overrule. Tap to OK
a 200% yearly increase in yoga slash meditation. Affluence
squandered to be *in the moment.* My mother gets the joke:
her age-achieved mastery; each morning her mind nearer
perfection. We laugh together at Alzheimer's paradox,
then moments later, sans irony, she asks: why the laughter?
Careful down the steps and don't forget your lunch box,
she reminded me fifteen hundred times, conservatively,
between first grade and junior high. Still, yesterday, late
for the gate, I observed my feet sliding out from under me
as I tumbled down the escalator, snack-pack taking flight.
Then panic as I pat the wrong pocket: Keys? iPhone? Wallet?
My life story is missing, my mother says. Who will tell it?

SWEET CAROLINE

From this distance you could be shooing flies, but as I exit
independent living to enter the memory-care unit

I can see, performing his Neil Diamond dip-shake-swivel,
the resident accordionist. According to Wiesenthal,

evil flourishes when the good do nothing, and the evidence
is everywhere. Yet from here, watching you dance

to the wheeze and bellow, a choir of cafeteria aides praising
your name with every chorus, I think of the arrays

of the brain, our synapsis endlessly reinventing us. *Dementia
is lessened by music therapy,* the director mentions,

which has potential to ameliorate your mother's depression.
And so, I watch you sway and clap, your expression,

unrecognizable, is—dare I say the word?—sweet. O Caroline,
may you who prized vinegar above honey—resigned

to life's bitter truths: a husband's murder, an indifferent God—
now, finally, sing: *good times never seemed so good.*

"MY DYING IS NOT TRAGIC"

my mother says, "so save your petitions and poems." If any god
is listening to her recitation of fanatical faith in the existence
of No God, I entreat Them to not misinterpret acquiescence
as contentment. "I will not," she mocks, "resurrect in a graveyard,
nor haunt your waking dreams. Every second," she explains,
"more than one hundred humans die; six hundred since I said
this last sentence. There will never be justice for these murdered
children, or their parents forever suffering unspeakable pain."
I'm in her hospital room, the TV blaring another school shooting;
officials offering thoughts and prayers. "My dying is not tragic,"
my mother repeats; adding, as if awed by nature's mathematics—
"my heart beat its wings four billion times" (she's computing
pulses per minute x years). Outside her window a hummingbird
hovers. "Miraculous," she whispers, as if sanctifying that word.

UNFORGETTABLE

I think of you every moment I say at my mother's unveiling
before setting stones on her stone, and kneeling

in the dirt. Behind me, my sister and two cousins murmur
assent. To our left, waiting patiently, my father,

his forty-fifth year underground. I cannot now recall that first
hour I thought of neither; perhaps I was nursing

a flu, head cloudy with Sudafed, body fatigued and fevered,
or maybe that morning when, surprised by my lover,

we feigned illness, indulging a matinee and, muting my phone,
I saw my feed feting a celebrity I hadn't known

was still alive. By then, of course, they weren't, having over-
dosed the day before, but still, it made me cover

my ears to better hear their unforgettable one-hit heartthrob
song I'd hummed since sixteen. *Thingamabob*

is what you christened everything that first chilly December
you forgot my father's name, and then my father.

UNVEILING

At the university in Tel Aviv, the scientists have printed
a miniature human heart. 3-D. Rabbit-sized, but replete—
the researcher used her own cells—with blood vessels,
mitral valves, ventricles, cava. When my mother's muscle
stopped beating, moments after I gave the surgical center
my written non-intervention permission, I became aware
for the first time of the warren of my body, its escape routes
and artificial enclosures. *No soul but soil* my mother taught
and it stuck; afterlife of neither God nor prayer, but pebble-
mud-dirt. And yet, one year to the day, my sister and I gather
graveside to recite, transliterated, the Mourner's Kaddish
after divesting the monument of its covering cloth. Ritual
complete we fold into vehicles, two emergency-medical-
cooler-torsos transporting home our holy, temporary hearts.

III

Reading Kafka to My Daughter

WHITE PRIVILEGE

Hiking the Joshua Tree trails, all thought, at first, deserts me—
newspaper politics, past due taxes, poetry; what favored luxury

allows this? Here is the hidden path where brothers Bill
and Jim formed the McHenry gang, rustling stolen cattle

from Arizona, and herding them to California for rebranding
before trading out East. Even their pastor praised upstanding

good-hearted-boys, unencumbered until civilization encroached.
Now my mind marches to today's Atlantic Coast, its tiki torches,

nooses, hoods, the internet of cities burning with a passion
that survived the doused fires. *Jew will not replace us* echoes

off the Black Rock Canyon walls of this Mohave ecosystem.
You'll never escape America's merciless history of 'isms,'

God whispers, as we sit among the wildflowers near the Oasis
of Mara. *I give you paradise, but all you ever write about is race,*

or sex, or class. Look around you for once at all I've offered:
the skull rock, the cottonwood spring; what greater suffering

denies the view from Key's Crest, or my easy loop at Barker Dam?
Once, on a far-away mountain, didn't I trick your father, Abraham,

toward, tangled in the thicket, my most privileged white ram?

TRUTH

"I was gypped," I'd cry to my mother after my older sister
divided the pie; "gypped," I'd say, counting out fifteen donuts
in the Sweet Sixteen bag. Fitzgerald imagined Myrtle's sister,
Catherine, "gypped" out of twelve hundred in Monte Carlo.
So, when the cultured Parisian gentleman murmured "don't Jew me"
during negotiations for the Richard Yarde watercolor portrait
of Sojourner Truth, I concocted a prior appointment and suggested
we reconvene after lunch. There at the corner of Park and Pine,
I took a minute to remember how Master Dumont told Belle,
age nineteen, she was his favorite slave, honest and strong,
and if she labored even harder, he would, in ten years' time,
release her. O, how she rejoiced—mowing, chopping, reaping, sowing—
each day was one day nearer to freedom. And when that dawn came
and Dumont claimed he'd changed his mind, Belle changed her name,
left her children behind and struck out under cover of darkness.
The Roma too escaped to a strange land, where they were mistaken
for Egyptians and disdained as thieving gypsies. Because names matter,
when my son rented a summer cottage, sixty miles from Manhattan—
just ten minutes from the beach—and I learned that in thirty-nine
Yaphank had an Adolph Hitler Street (now Pine) and that there was
still a German Gardens Park and Camp Siegfried, I urged him not
to sign the lease. But when I last visited, he was in the front yard
relaxing with a Lowenbrau and *The Great Gatsby*. Sojourner
never drank nor could she read, but she traveled north sharing
the Lord's love, and rarely sleeping. Which makes me embarrassed
to admit how tired I am right now as I sit down on the grass
surrounding the Truth Memorial sculpture. I can almost hear her

booming voice, as if it were eighteen fifty-three, proclaiming
"I will come out and tell you what time o' night it is." Because
words matter, I listen, transfixed until she's finished, surprised,
when I open my eyes, that the sun has set, and it's already evening.

COWARD

chicano kid racing   the wrong way
and i'm counting off   cop seconds
wondering   from whose perspective
it's the rose bowl   in twenty-nine and
there's riegels in   his own end zone
arms raised like goalposts   or surrender
not yet knowing the game is over   and over
there some white girl   aiming like a gun
at the asian boy running   interference for or
is he this close to sacking   the purse-snatcher
he's a hero   they wrote in the newspapers
though i can't recall if it was   the man shot
in the back or the man   who did the shooting
in my life i've always been a coward   except
that one time when i saw   the black guy pinch
the baby and right in front of me   tuck her in
under his arm and head down   head downtown
while the woman squeals   and i take flight
like a bullet and make the flying tackle   who
wouldn't hand off that baby and   run i yell
wrestling him back down don't move   hearing
his bones crack and panting panting come the police
who later that day release   the child's father
who'd tracked down   his kidnapped daughter
through three time-zones till now   and me

READING KAFKA TO MY DAUGHTER

It was a second-grade sleepover in the open space
recently renovated above our garage, and seven
seven-year-old girls dizzying their bodies in the way
a story consumes the one spinning it, a chrysalis
of choice and misdirection until you emerge
unrecognizable even to yourself. It happened
that I was in the basement reading *The Metamorphosis*
when my wife got the call from her mother and left me
alone—well not alone—one of eight in the house
before bedtime. So it came to pass that I, rolling out
the plastic mat with the wide colored circles, stood
among shrieks and giggles, as the numerous, if pitifully
thin limbs transmuted—left foot red, right hand green—
into a single multi-headed over-tired insect.
But that—the incessant shape-shifting of our forms
and minds is not what I wanted to say. Nor is this poem
about the calls my wife fielded all of the following week
about the inappropriateness of reading Kafka—
how could he?—to prepubescents. No. I share this
only to better remember the morning after the nightmare,
when I went to wake them, their tangled intentions
and odd dreams twisted protectively around each other,
then, suddenly, like a field of sunflowers, each tilted
her face toward the skylight, petals extended upward
as if stretching to touch daybreak's bright yellow sphere.

NOBODY

The day I played Emily in drag on an Amherst stage
I finally understood the slant of my ambition. Desire
entered my body like variant words scrawled sideways
on a repurposed envelope. Inside was the flaming soul
of her fame. I adjusted my wig as the audience roared.
Outside, the snow—*sent us of the air*—was again falling
when a gust flung open the hallway door. There she was,
a ghost haunting the Homestead gift store. *I'm Nobody*
T-shirts hung beside illustrated guestbooks, and DVDs.
I tried to tell her that 233 biographies were available on
Amazon, but she'd already turned toward the stairwell,
disregarding the nameless crowd and my unconvincing
juvenile humor. *Love me,* she mouthed. She shared no
other words. So, I echoed—*love me*—even as I climbed
to her refurbished bedroom and stared out the window
at those feathered twin Seraphim, Hope and Despair.

VICTIM MENTALITY

I'm writing about Hitler's Aunt Johanna who, visiting
her sister's house to greet her newborn nephew, offers
to watch baby Adolph while Klara gets a necessary rest
after a welcome but difficult delivery; when my mother,
wiping away tears, interrupts. She's searching for tissues
as she tells me why she wishes that the little Negro girl—
the one she reads to as part of the senior-center program
to aid the disadvantaged—had picked a different picture
book; the Pinkney-Lester one was about slavery and why
let that delicious child grow up with a victim's mentality?
After all, haven't we had an African-American president,
and did you ever hear talk of the Holocaust in our house?
That's why you turned out happy, she continues, and well-
adjusted, although God knows, even you have your issues.

LITERATURE OF THE BODY

What a time we live in, my mother says. She's reading
that the human genome's three billion genetic "letters"
can map each organism's DNA. But haven't I got enough
tsuris wrestling with these miserable twenty-six that
can't even solve the simplest puzzle of love's meaning?
Not to mention the question of passion, which smells,
as my *bubbe* explained to my *zayde* on their wedding day,
like an altogether different *tshaynik* of fish. And because
they didn't wake up as one, or worse, two of six million,
my anxiety, I suppose, is still predisposed for flight. Why
else keep one eye open all night and my sole good ear
tuned to approaching danger. A stranger comes to town
or our hero goes on a journey, I learned in Junior High,
were our civilization's only plots. With more than one-
hundred-thousand-thousand words in the English language
and a drizzle of Yiddish on top, you'd think there'd be
greater variety between generations. But here I am, quiet
as death, writing my life, and sleeping as fast as I can.

THE FIRST QUESTION

I see you, my young mother says, removing her palms
from my eyes, as I watch myself squeal with delight—
or appear to in silent eight-millimeter black and white,
since transferred to VHS to DVD to Digital. Now, calm
again, I stare at the lens, my father's unexpected splurge,
as he focuses on our future, recording my past. *I see you*
the mechanical eye whirrs, adjusting its peripheral view
to my father's murder, my mother's dementia, merging
time with diminishment. *What do we want but to be seen
and not suffer,* my mother says, addressing my camera
before being wheeled into the ICU. *Where are you, ayeka*
the All-Knowing-God queries Adam. *What do you mean,*
I call out, too late, as I tally my sins, fearing abandonment.
I am hiding, Adam answers, his every breath, a sacrament.

LANGUAGE

My first syllables were Silence, though I am gifted in Self
and have been mistaken for a native speaker. God says a field
of sunflowers in Death Valley and I translate the Brooklyn
gutter of my father's murder. I avoid the cliché, Holocaust,
substituting colitis. That is my genius. No, listen, God says,
you are missing the local accent, the surf in Nosara at six a.m.—
the sound of it, the consistency of forgiveness. But I am seeing
my grandfather shoved into the cattle car, and later shoveled
out of the chamber. The dull and paralyzing music. There is no
other way to phrase it. *Yes*, to art celebrating our fragile lives,
and each individual's anguish. A song or a symphony. A poem.
So, we transform words. Find the nuance. There is no God,
I tell you, but listen to my breath, your breath. Like the sea
we are water and all of us beautiful. Let us be silent together.

ELECTROCUTING MONKEYS

The power line that brings light to the village
passes uninsulated through the Costa Rican
jungle. I'm in our hotel, dreaming of Zuniga—
his full-bodied madonnas and his matriarchs
of unshakeable faith—when I'm awakened
by the Howler; her hellish ear-splitting growl
outside my window. She's swinging tree to tree
seeking fresh leaves, while below, at the beach,
newly hatched turtles journey from sand nest
to ocean. We hike down, anxiously waving arms
at the vultures circling overhead. You explain
that only one in over one-hundred-thousand egg-
aphrodisiacs will result in a mature leatherback.
And so, I carry a shell to the water's edge and set
that single life safely beneath the waves. We swim
in a frenzy of hatchlings, and not a fish net in sight.
We're government-and-God-protected. The night,
they still tell us, is harmless, is sleeping, is silent.

EVEN LIGHT CANNOT ESCAPE

Sudden, the newspaper says, and unexpected; no cause
listed before your final bow. Suicide, I assume, because

no malignancy mentioned. Yet you called yourself blessed
to see the mountains of piled rocks daily from your guest's

bedroom windows; sacred sands of a desert floor. A miracle,
I agreed, emerging from the healing waters of a hot mineral

cure. How little I knew of your life: bed and breakfast host,
trail guide, gay, married, and today, before driving west,

my wife scanning the Mohave Sun, mouths your name; a name,
now carved by the blunt knife of my memory into the arms

of every Joshua Tree. There you are, last week, protesting
the short-term, short-sighted Trump government shutdown,

park rangers sidelined, as vandals tagged these time-travelers—
boulders and bark—from an earlier age. How brief and fragile

our bodily lives, how petty this need for remembrance. Here,
trending on my feed, photographs of a black hole, the power

of nature from fifty-five million light-years; a one-way portal
to eternity. The door unlocked, we find the key on the mantle,

and next to your welcome note, a flickering flame, a candle

POEM CORRECTING CONJECTURE
IN THE PREVIOUS POEM

Heart attack, I've heard, after, on a community stage
your final bow. Sudden and unexpected. No raging

against God or self, except by exaggerated farcical script.
Death then, was no blessed release, no furtive addiction.

In school we played at *Fire and Ice*, Frost's poem, by rote,
made classroom game. I raised my hand, the Holocaust

just one more choice. Gas, rope, knife, pill; the bullet
that the ravaged body begs for, and the one that killed

my father—both the same. Einstein prophesied that time
and space would disappear *forever*; each, victim

of a cosmic violence—the host ingesting itself from within.
The newspaper says you are survived by two Seussian-

named Schnoodles (their picture featured), plus a husband,
niece, stepmother, many friends. What better ending

would we wish ourselves than this, painless and swift,
after acting the wise fool. Black holes, the physicists insist

are ringed—water orbiting a drain—by luminescent circles.
The rabbis say the Lord Himself cannot suffocate a soul.

Today, hiking your favored path, sunlight on sand, an angel

PROSPECTUS

...didn't say enough about hedge funds or real estate development.
    —From a one-star review of my poetry collection,
    More Money than God, on Goodreads

I say in the beginning was the word. I say sell. Or hold. The jet-setters
will gentrify anyway, kicking the poets curbside. I say God's grammar
cannot be valued like bitcoins on eBay. Consider how literature stammered
its way from cuneiform to computer code, yet all language favors debtors

over lenders. I ask what can we learn from the brokers and go-getters?
Even in my old Brooklyn tenement, the rent subsidized tenants know
meaning is derivative, not variable. I say think ink as cash. A steady flow
stimulates the brain. Imagination, not markets, must remain unfettered

and free. I say screw obscurity. It's true James Merrill had two Irish Setters
and a country estate (I've parsed each word of my Merrill-Lynch prospectus),
but neither wealth nor art are hedge against death; that truth connects us—
though each thinks his path the better—whether we're of means or of letters.

YES, THE MESSIAH

*When the messiah comes if He says nice to meet you the Christians will
apologize to the Jews. If He says nice to see you again, the Jews will apologize
to the Christians.*

    —Amos Oz's grandmother

There is Moses of Crete and Moses of Cisneros, and even a case
could be made for the majestic Hebrew. How does one choose
between the fraudulent world and its small promises? Comfort
or pleasure? False Messiah or family reunion? Even my aunt
rails against the graven images of Elvis Presley's immortality,
steering the conversation back toward *Der Stürmer*'s fat-bellied,
hook-nosed, killers of Christ. *Holy Cow! They find hate funny,*
my thick-lipped uncle says, waving a butt-naked, ass-up cartoon
Mohammed. But why debate? We all have our claims and I too
have lost the truth between my life and its story. *Yes, the messiah,*
my grandmother sighs, and so let us all follow her to the edge
of the ocean. Let us wait forever and celebrate our divinity. Let us
apologize to each other, whether or not the waters begin to rise.

IV

Turtle of Slow Devotion

TURTLE OF SLOW DEVOTION

Eleven Prayers for Passover

i. PASSOVER PRAYER (WITH HOUSE PETS)

Belief is the cat scratching at the back-screen door,
wanting in, wanting out, sipping from the goblet
of wine we left for Elijah, too near the water bowl.
Faith is the stray dog rescued, his slobbering tongue
both trial and proof. Each day, he waits dutifully,
confident of your return. Trust is the parakeet kept
caged and covered inside our faintly beating hearts.
O turtle of slow devotion, gerbil of circular reasoning,
let patience be our exercise wheel; and this prayer
the bathwater, steadily rising, until even the goldfish
of my misgivings swim past window-sash and door-
post, the house overflowing with chaos, with awe.

ii. PRAYER BEFORE THE WASHING OF THE HANDS

I wash my hands of you, my grandmother bellowed,
but I was feeling superior to the gaudy housedress
pattern of her dictates, and her superstitious slippers
so, when the curse caught itself on a protruding screw
of my high school chair where I sat studying *Macbeth*
and analyzing his Lady, I didn't even look up. It was
only later, back home, before the dipping of the *karpas*
when she pointed out the dribble of blood on my finger
that I let her cradle the backs of my hands in her hands
until she could re-balance the weight of transgression
versus virtue, guiding my palms together as if she were
the scholar and I the one praying in front of God's gate.

iii. PRAYER BEFORE THE DIPPING OF THE HERBS

Let us dip the fresh herbs and spring vegetables
into the cups full with the tears of our mothers,
who dipped their own greens into the cupped hands
that held their mothers' tears. We can track mothers
back to their place of origin, the spring from which
the stream arose to nourish the arid landscape I see out
the window of the house where we gather every spring
to celebrate our freedom. But there, sneaking off to attack
go the generals, their imaginations corrupted by survival
or power, like stories stored in an ancient computer file
we can no longer access. So let the children push back
their chairs from the table and grow up to misremember
these explosions as the sound of the Angel of Reparations
wrestling with the Angel of Peace. Let the winner's wings
sprout new growth until, too heavy to fly, they take root,
become shade trees, each leaf an unanswered question.

iv. PRAYER BEFORE THE BREAKING OF THE MATZO

And if we must be broken, let us be broken
like the *afikoman,* that hidden shard of matzo
cherished above the whole. Let us be wrapped
in the soft linen napkin of the Lord's silence
like pilgrims kneeling on smooth stones
in a Jerusalem gutter, oblivious to the clatter
of the market. Let our children, searching
beneath cushions, call out to claim lost quarters.
Let them ransom us back to the table.

v. PRAYER BEFORE THE TELLING OF THE STORY

I will create as I speak, God's Names say.
But we, who own only these twenty-six
symbols to express our every possibility
must wrestle with speech as if language
was Jacob's Angel. So, let us now pray,
even as did thick-tongued Moses, ever el-
oquent within Michelangelo's solid block
of marble but rendered mute by his escape.

vi. PRAYER BEFORE THE ASKING OF THE QUESTIONS

Clever was what we'd hoped to be called,
too young to consider kindness as an option.
O wicked and wise brothers, unknowing and
innocent sisters, let us weep together once more
in the supermarket aisle of our pre-adolescence,
let us cry out, overwhelmed by the choices—

Mama?

Papa?

—each of us praying we'll be the prodigal,
prized beyond the steadfast. *Clever children,*
God says, scooping us back into the basket.

vii. PRAYER BEFORE THE PARTING OF THE SEA

Let us praise those abandoned on the shore,
unsure of the trick of their eyes, but knowing
in their hearts that the waters will refuse to part.
They are standing there still, calculating tides,
and measuring mud flats; their flow charts
and bridges deserving no lesser suspension
of disbelief. May we watch our brethren pass-
over daily, their encouragements drowned
in the sound of the armies descending upon us.
Death's certainty, too, is a kind of miracle.

viii. PRAYER BEFORE THE SLAYING OF THE FIRST BORN

And if we who are your replacements refuse to praise
the slaughter? And if, refusing, we forget to bloody
our doorposts? And if, forgetting, we turn our
backs to the window and never see God's
curtain of merciful light slowly lowered
like a plague of darkness before us?
Tonight, let my thoughts swarm
like locusts, devouring reason.
Let my heart be an army
of leaping frogs.

ix. PRAYER BEFORE THE EATING OF THE KORECH

Between the petitions God hears, and then refuses to hear, Hillel sits.
Between the faithful, and the passionate appeals-filing law clerks,
Hillel sits. Between the *not now*, and the *then when*, Hillel sits.

Between his ancient, bitter Babylonian grandmother and her
democratic-socialist-twentieth-century-post-Holocaust descendants,
Hillel sits. So tonight, let us approach our tables like a jury of peers.

Let us neither judge, nor fill our plates with the dark sweet paste of regret.
Let us follow our prayers to the empty chair between the Angel of All
We Will Never Know, and the Angel of All We Must Never Forget.

x. PRAYER BEFORE THE PEELING OF THE EGG

And if we must be broken,
let us be broken like this hairline cracked shell
with its web-patterned tendrils of doubt. Let us lift
the perfect eleven from their protective pulp-molded embrace
as if HaShem Herself had displaced them from our savior's table.
Fragile and fractured we enter the world, carried home
in Moses's basket. Above us the burnt roasted egg
of a moon, inside us the accusatory
quiet eye of its yolk.

xi. PRAYER BEFORE THE SLAUGHTER OF THE LAMB

Let the lion circle its prey while we place the violin
under the chins of our children, guiding their fingers
along its slender tapered maple neck. Let the tough
connective tissues tear, tendons ripped by the grip
of teeth, while we tighten rosewood pegs, admire
the luthier's skill in the carved decorative scroll.
What is the resonance, my lamb, of civilization,
and how many lives will we willingly sacrifice?
There is blood on our doorposts, fright and bleat,
but let us now be as farmers planting, each pitch
a single seed. May this note blossom into prayer.

MEDITATION BEFORE THE SAYING OF THE PRAYERS

And where was God before creating the universe or
the minds of men, my son's Sunday school teacher
is asking the third-grade class as I arrive with the box
of cupcakes my wife baked for the world's birthday.
Hands shoot up—me, me—lips pleading. This is what
supplication sounds like, I want to tell the instructor,
but she, I can now see, is not much more than a child
herself. So let me personify perplexity and schmear
my mouth with chocolate. Let me stand here empty-
handed in front of the room, indiscernible as all being
before the word, or time's creation, waiting for prayer.

MEDITATION BEFORE THE SPINNING OF THE DREIDEL

You're spiraling out of control, my father
warns me, he who is himself still swirling
around his own father who has been orbiting
the earth for forty years, flying from pogrom
to pogrom, touching ground only to praise
each grandson's birth. And how busy God
must be to keep the planets rotating, His grin
strained as that of the circus plate spinner
I loved to watch on Ed Sullivan. If He slows,
even momentarily, who knows how long
before history would wobble, toppling over
and killing us all, or half, or none. Are you in?
God asks. Yes? Then let the spinning begin.

BREAKFAST ELEGY FOR A SURVIVOR

Paperbacks still stacked on the tilt-top tray, spines splayed open;
silenced by your death, these pre-coital or post-murder lovers.
And piled bedside, a mawkish feast of tawdry colored covers
I'd mocked as empty calories. *Like orange juice, heavy with pulp,
is how I favor my fictions,* you parried, pouring us each a tumbler.
And so, I recommended a more nutritious diet—serious tomes
and higher art—defending my taste for Raskolnikov over Holmes
(Celan, Bach, Rembrandt above doggerel, ditty, paint by number).
Great literature breeds empathy, I insisted, citing the *New York Times*
and resting my case. *Let's drink to Shakespeare, a genius of rhymes,*
you countered, raising your glass. *Hitler, too, was an ardent admirer.
His Jew of Venice was vellum-bound and swastika embossed*
(it was the first and only time you'd alluded to the Holocaust).
And then we clinked, and you picked up your *National Enquirer.*

LIFE SENTENCE

A "Holocaust Jew" my grandfather calls me. And not kindly.
My identity defined by the negative; not passion, not mystery,
not awe before the great unknown, but the burden of history
and fear. Politics above prayer, stuck on the picket line, blindly
following, he says, the atheists, and unenlightened masses.
No arguing *where was your God when* . . . when love is not logic.
And so I embrace denial, and make my nest from the tragic,
twig by twig, starving the songbird of my heart till joy passes.
Then today, observing his *yahrzeit*, a small peep of repentance—
call it delight—escapes my lips as the candle's smoke assumes
the form of Hillel, great sage who crafted from words our tombs
and hammered Torah, his truth and life, into a single sentence—
What is hateful to you, do not do unto others—a text for every age.
But too soon the flame is mute; my mind again consumed by rage.

LISTENING TO THE NAMES—SIMCHAT TORAH 2020

I.

Listening to the names shouted at the Black Lives Matter
Rally: Breonna, George, Tamir, I think of my grandfather
chanting each weekly Torah *parashah* until all seventy-nine
thousand, eight-hundred and forty-seven words are recited;
it takes a year, he'd explain, to complete the pronunciation
of the full name of God. Today, all around me, I hear lovers
sobbing and fathers praying for Sandra, Alatiana, Rayshard,
Daniel, Michelle, Freddie, their names written with black fire
on white fire, each letter seared into air and heart and stone.
Murder Not saith the Lord before ordering Moses to slaughter
innocent Midianites, unleashing millennia of erudite exegesis
on the translation of a single Hebrew word. O Aura, Philando,
Alton, Akai, Stephon, I hear you on the sidewalks, in the parks,
driving your cars, home in bed as you plead for your mothers
and beg your deities, repeating one name and then the other
as we now shout out yours: Eric, Tanisha, Janisha. O Emmett,
forever fourteen, let me tell you, you who should be seventy-
nine in this New Year of 5781, that tonight is Simchat Torah
when the scrolls will be taken from the ark as we worshippers
dance and drink and sing with abandon until the dawn breaks
and the final verse of Deuteronomy is followed by the opening
chapter of Genesis, both completing and beginning the cycle.

II.

If Torah is the blood of God, then let our names be God's body:
Abel, Absalom, Er, Onan. Maurice, my father, Moishe, Morrie,
Moe. Mickey, Mike murdered (see *ratzah*, רצח the Hebrew root,
as opposed to *harag* הרג, to kill, as in capital punishment, stand
your ground, ritual slaughter, temple sacrifice) for no crime but
living in the wrong neighborhood, worshipping the wrong God
which was no God at all. And now writing our ancestors' names
in black ink on white paper, I let the flames consume themselves
before reading aloud: Solomon, Ina, Micha, Mordecai massacred
by the Polish Policja; Rachel, Yochanan, Esther, and Shmuel shot
by the Schutzstaffel (literally: *The Protection Squadron*). Blessing
the children of Israel before his death, Moses addressed each soul
individually. *What do we want but to be known and remembered?*
There are twenty-four hundred and fifteen proper names in Torah
my grandfather instructs, and every year we must restate them all.
Today, sixty years later, I realize I still do not know how to listen.
Speak, my mother once told me, *only if what you have need to say
is more beautiful than silence.* Every breath is both a transgression
and prayer. Let us live in the space between letters, between the act
and its judgment. Botham, Michael, Kayla, Asher, let us assemble
and listen to the names. Those we love most will soon all be gone.
Begin again. *Be strong, be strong, and let us strengthen each other.*

THE TORAH SCRIBE'S RIDDLE

Plucked from a chicken, the left-wing flight-feathered quill
will be his fingers' first partner for this dance of survival,
this bi-millennial perfectly choreographed dip, spin, and swivel,
till all three hundred and four thousand, eight hundred and five
letters are complete; a trot and tango of statutes, stories, and begats.
Let the metal forgers, the woodworkers, the carvers of limestone
compete with their statues of this lower-case deity, or that.
"Shall we pray to a ceramic bird head or to *The Great Unknown?*"
he asks me, who stopped by for neither idle nor idol chatter,
but to see the parchments sewn and to learn to mix the ink.
I ask how animal veins are dried for thread, but he is undeterred.
"Absurd, your attempt to learn the skill without loving the matter
he scolds. Do we not create ourselves as we transcribe, think,
and debate? Now I ask you which came first: God or The Word?"

MEDITATION ON THE MURDER OF THE OVERSEER

...and he spied an Egyptian smiting an Hebrew. And he looked this way and that way, and when he saw no man, he slew the Egyptian, and hid him in the sand.

    —Exodus 2:11-12

Not murder, we tell our sons, but the overcoming of oppression.
Not murder, we tell our daughters, but a direct argument against
institutional racism. Not sin, Moses explains, since God hadn't yet
emblazoned ten edicts in stone. Ex *post facto*, God says, sentencing
twenty years' probation, doubled for doubt and innuendo. And here
they remain, three millennia later, still quarreling inside my brain
like Hillel and Shammai parsing points of law while, sequestered,
I'm sitting in judgment between the snake and the rod; my heart,
that helpless Pharaoh, hardening inside me. *My Dad was murdered*
is what I thought I'd heard through the static, but I kept chattering
about second chances, the blood-red sea, and the hot desert sand.
Did thine enemy not save you before they enslaved you, the Lord
once enquired. We were at a crossroad, and so I looked this way
and then that way before I reached out and offered up my hand.

MEDITATION AFTER CASTING
MY SINS UPON THE WATERS

As if God had kicked the crutch of belief out from under
the limbs of the wounded. As if our souls were unwanted
weekend guests in the summer beach house of the body.
As if I were still the magician's pre-pubescent assistant,
waving my skinny arm and wand. *I Will Create as I Speak*
the Lord once saith, in Aramaic no less—*Avra Kahdabra*—
distracting us with cape and hat and that sly, cunning grin.
O how I envied His deep voice and gift for misdirection.
And now my astonishment at this morning's small miracle
when, up early and stumbling at the shore, I saw, as I fell
face down into the shallows, my sins swimming about me
like a school of minnows, no, I mean like my own fingers,
all ten of them, intertwining into a gesture of prayer.

Coda

RECIPE

At the bakery, the bread is free, but the poem recited
before bagging each loaf costs six dollars. A stratagem
to celebrate life. Add water, leaven, and let the hymn,
the canticle, the psalm, rise in your throat. Uninvited
to my own party I didn't realize that the heavenly choir
singing the cacophony of arguments inside my head
was only the quiet couple next-door quarreling in bed;
what my mother would call a certain recipe for disaster.
Of course, everyone deserves health care, shelter, food,
even sexual satisfaction. I used to believe in intelligence;
now my wife wants to add loving-kindness into the mix.
Do we need to hear more from our gods or less? Odd,
how laughter's portions are larger on the poorest menu.
Lord, give us the strength to feed each other and continue.

Acknowledgements

Grateful acknowledgment is made to the editors of the following journals and anthologies in which poems first appeared, sometimes in earlier versions.

Anthologies

"Fake News" and "Gossip is Forbidden," *What Saves Us: Poems of Empathy and Outrage in the Time of Trump*, Northwestern University Press, 2019.

"Meditation after Casting My Sins Upon the Waters," *Wild Gods*, New Rivers Press, 2021.

"Prayer Before the Eating of the Korech," *New Voices: Contemporary Writers Confronting the Holocaust*, Vallentine Mitchell, 2023.

"Truth," *Compass Roads: Poems about the Pioneer Valley*, Levellers Press, 2018.

Journals

"The Wedding in the Cemetery" and "Vermin": *The Common*.

"Nobody": *Emily Dickinson Society Newsletter*.

"Bless You" and "The Torah Scribe's Riddle": *The Hopkins Review*.

"White Privilege" and "Open Carry": *The Massachusetts Review*

"A Horse-Cure," "Life Sentence," "What My Mother Remembers—Memorial Day," "I Create as I Speak," "What My Mother Remembers—New Year's Day," "My Dying is not Tragic," "Unveiling": *Nimrod*.

"Maybe the Messiah": *On the Seawall*.

"Language" and "Life Sentence": *Shirim: A Jewish Poetry Journal*.

"Envisioning the Life, Post-Parole, of my Father's Murderer": *Solstice*.

"Venery": *Tikkun*.

"Angels with Guns Guarding the Gates of Heaven": *Vox Populi*.

A debt of gratitude to poets Martin Espada, Paul Mariani, and Lesléa Newman for your support and friendship over the years; and to the poets in Group 18 who helped me craft many of these poems: Doug Anderson, Bob Coles, Trish Crapo, Roz Driscoll, Paul Dubois Jacobs, Margaret Lloyd, Henry Lyman, Missy-Marie Montgomery, Bill O'Connell, Anne Love Woodhull. I am lucky to have good friends who are renowned actors: thanks to Raye Birk, Candace Barrett Birk, Jay O. Sanders, Maryann Plunkett, and Gabor Barabas for bringing some of the poems in this collection to life. Thanks also to the editors of my previous collections, Laurence Lieberman at the University of Illinois Press, and Ed Ochester at the University of Pittsburgh Press, for keeping me going, and especially to Gregory Wolfe at Slant Books for giving me, and so many authors I admire, a new home in his Republic of Letters.

This book was set in Centaur, designed by the American typographer and book designer, Bruce Rogers, who was commissioned to create an exclusive type for the Metropolitan Museum of Art (New York) in 1914. Based on the Renaissance-period printing of Nicolas Jenson around 1470, it was named Centaur after the title of the first book designed by Rogers using the type: The Centaur by Maurice de Guérin, published in 1915. Lanston Monotype of London cut the commercial version of Centaur and released it in 1929.

This book was designed by Shannon Carter, Ian Creeger, and Gregory Wolfe. It was published in hardcover, paperback, and electronic formats by Slant Books, Seattle, Washington.

Cover photo: Jurien Huggins, Unsplash.

CPSIA information can be obtained
at www.ICGtesting.com
Printed in the USA
JSHW022114060623
42810JS00003B/175